Lynda —

with tremendous
gratitude for writing my
endorsement for my
book — and for your importa
work in the world.

Peace,
Pam Ballingham
10-6-18

Praise for Tributaries: A Book of Poetry

"Pamala Ballingham's work makes a significant contribution to the Great Work of our time – in these poems she listens to the hidden voices of the world and sings them back in intimate and beautiful words that bring us into deeper connection with all of life."

> Lyanda Fern Lynn Haupt
> Author of *Mozart's Starling, and Crow Planet*

"Pamala Ballingham has a unique quality that allows her to join heart and mind in a way we can all resonate with. For her, mind becomes a vehicle for the heart to sing its songs in a language that penetrates to the very core of the listener. Her poems are genuine heart-to-heart communications, imbued with a deep spirituality that brings us face to face with the great mystery of Being. I find myself savoring them, digesting them, then going back for another serving!"

> Upasaka Culadasa (John Yates, PhD)
> Author of *The Mind Illuminated: A Complete Guide Using Buddhist Wisdom and Brain Science,* Director of Dharma Treasure Buddhist Sangha

"Pamala's poems are tributaries in the greater stream of a poetic tradition that is deeply rooted in the natural world and informed by a spiritual understanding that places the reader in that world – the only world we have."

> Larry Robinson
> Founder and producer of Rumi's Caravan, poet, author of *Roll Away The Stone,* retired Eco-psychologist

"A lifetime of involvement with Native practices and Buddhist meditation has prepared Pamala uniquely for this calling. Can you hear it? The silence of the Sonoran desert speaks directly through her."

> Shinzen Young
> Author of *The Science of Enlightenment: How Meditation Works,* neuroscience research consultant

"Playful, powerful, perfect. The descriptions held in each beautiful piece tantalize the senses for the young and old alike."

> Pauline Wilson
> Poet and educator

"Pamala Ballingham brings her years of wisdom, travel, and spirituality into this treasured collection of poetry. Her imagery at once gives you chills and makes you chuckle. The meter is so well-crafted and so playful that I find I can only read, and reread, these poems out loud."

Tucker Peck
PhD, Licensed Clinical Psychologist, Director of
Palo Santo Psychotherapy & Wellness, and Pragmatic Dharma
Teacher

"Poignant verses delicately bridge the heart and mind in visually captivating descriptions. Pamala Ballingham skillfully connects the reader to beauty, wonder, joy and love of life through her words. There is a poem, poetic story, or haiku for everyone."

M. Bond
Author of five books, co-author of two

"This collection of poems is an incredible feast for all the senses. Allow yourself to be taken on a magical ride of emotions, times, and places that will touch your very core."

Theresa Landow
Author

"This engaging book of free verse, story poems and a chapter of haiku takes the reader on a spiritual journey of mystical and natural exploration. The journey begins by awakening the senses to piñon pines and places far away. These poems have undertones of grief and loss with an even greater understanding of the natural order and beauty within the circle of life."

Shaman Vitki
NewAgeBooksReview. com

"Each page of *Tributaries* offers a magical invitation to see the world with awe. The gentleness and emotion leave me yearning for more."

Alisha Wilson
Business owner

TRIBUTARIES

A Book of Poetry

Pamala Ballingham

© 2018 Pamala Ballingham

Published by Earth Mother Productions

PO Box 43204 Tucson, AZ 85733

www.earthmotherproductions.com

Earth Mother Productions

ISBN: 0-922104-36-0

ISBN 13: 9780922104369

Library of Congress Control Number: **2017919126**
Earth Mother Productions, Tucson AZ.

FIRST EDITION

Printed in the United States of America

Cover and title page, *Leaves and Feathers*, painting by Pamala Ballingham, 2006

Drawings by Pamala Ballingham

Layout design, photography and painting, page 79, by Tim Ballingham

To

Tim Ballingham,
for whom love, generosity, and kindness
are words not large enough.

Ruth Schobert Harvey,
who pointed me in the direction of the Muse.

Chester Hewitt Harvey
and Katherine Armstrong,
whose dedicated engagement with the natural world
has been an inspiration.

George William Ballingham,
who has always been there with a ladder
and his box of handmade chocolates.

I think over again my small adventures,

my fears, the small ones that seemed so big,

of all the vital things I had to get and to reach and yet

there is only one great thing, the only thing—

to live to see the great day that dawns

and the light that fills the world.

—An old Inuit song

CONTENTS

ACKNOWLEDGMENTS

Tim Ballingham's wise counsel, technical skills, and
logistical mastery were indispensable.

I thank my editor, Deborah Beaumont, whose valuable assistance
was essential to the completion of this book.

Mysti Bond's expertise, creativity and energy for this project have been boundless.

Janet Davis was an essential source of encouragement and support throughout.

Nikki Westra and Eileen Jackson's sharp and discerning eyes
arrived at the perfect time.

Deepest gratitude to my wise and generous teacher,
Upasaka Culadasa (John Yates, PhD)

Many thanks to the following people who, each in his or her special way, added to
the spirit and substance of the poems:
Margarita Acosta
Allegra Ahlquist
Mad Bear Anderson
Deborah Arnold
Doug Boyd
Karen Vyner-Brooks
Chuong
Larry Elsner
Charlene Fiddler
Chenoa Fiddler
Hayward Fox, PhD
Miriam Furst
Jhan Kold
Mickey McDonald, M.D.
Eleanor Bingham Miller
Lee Stanfield
Tlakaelel
Adrian Van Suchtelen
Joanne Weiner
Renate Wygnanski
Nancy Yates
My creative, energetic students

PREFACE

The Muse, that untrimmable creative force, makes her presence known when she pulls me from sleep to sit under the silent moon or to watch with excitement as wind whips through trees in a storm. At such moments, it might prompt me to write a poem, compose a song, or inspire a form in clay. Something magical is at play here.

The Muse arrives unexpectedly and on her own terms. Once as I watched my husband, Tim, throw a mizusashi on the potter's wheel, his hands smothered in wet, glistening clay as the form rose up as if from primordial soup, the moment was ripe. I sensed something infinitely larger than the object being created, the potter, or me. At such times, I perceive an invisible interface between what we see and what actually exists had we a wider, wiser sensory system. Something lives between the ones and the zeros, weaving itself between what we believe are the fixed borders of our reality and a realm that is interactive and flexible. An object "more air than earth" is the porcelain bowl I made which emits this paradox when its delicate, wavy edges flicker and move with the changing light of day and the mercurial shadows of night. This phenomenon is reflected in the poem "Tea Ceremony." Here, accoutrements to the ancient ceremony play a traditionally prescribed role yet each moves in concert to invoke an essence that can't be precisely explained. To attempt proximity is dicey work.

There is sculpture in music and dance in words. These expressive tools, among many others, mix and move as the Muse plays in the studio of the mind with energy and fluidity. As I wrote, these poems shaped me as much as I shaped them. Some came like dance choreography in slow motion and some came as streaks of light. Regardless how they arose, I tend to experience the Muse as a shy and unpredictable creature who might arrive if discreetly massaged. My task is to prepare the landing strip.

Lastly, Tim woke up one morning from the nether world of sleep with the poem "Once We Were Trapped" on his lips. I can't resist including it. It is insightful, as he is, and is accompanied by his painting.

1

IN PLACES FAR AWAY

IN PLACES FAR AWAY

In places far away,
have you seen
the splintered silver bones of piñon trees
scattered beneath thickets of late summer green,

places only drifters know
where the air is pure and velvet,
without walls, sometimes
not even the wind,

places where silence moves
among great assemblages of trees
woven at the roots in vast familial webs,
calling you into rare and sacred spaces,
pulling you into the blue sage of the land

the kind old Utes once used
to brew medicine tea to clean festering wounds
suffered by lives torn from the land?

In gratitude for safe passage,
a small, desolate band
gave white buckskin gloves to Grandfather Albert,
massaged to perfection by worn-down, tired teeth,
the sacrificial gift the likes of which
we don't know anymore.

Have you seen
the splintered silver bones of piñon trees
scattered beneath thickets of late summer green?

MORNING RAVEN

Every morning
just beyond the fence line,
one lone raven
flies in desperation
toward the rising sun.

She circles south,
squawking at the world
in angry staccato,
announcing she has arrived,
then disappears back into the west,
leaving a vacuum of sound
in her wake.

Perhaps she's lost her mate
and been exiled from her constable,
left to restlessly search
this lonely quadrant,
a vagabond
flying for her life—
for the one possibility
that might work her back
into this narrow sliver of the world.

WITHOUT A WORD BEING SPOKEN
For Renate

What impotent little words
can I stitch together to say
how the granite-gray mountains
settle in the bone
when I first open the morning door?

Maybe the voice of Raven,
raspy like a tooth,
says it best
when she and her kin
piece together sound bites,
bird to bird,
like they have since the first sun.

Or maybe the pine tree
murmurs it most true
as she stands there, ecstatic,
her shining wings touching the sun,
her great roots in webs of woody rivers,
communing,
running off the mountain into the valley,
winding down the dusty road
and over the threshold.

I'll light a candle
that you, so far away,
can know it
without a word being spoken.

HIGH ESTES AFTERNOON

Thunderous winds
race through jagged gorges, chilling
as they spill over late-summer snowfields, while,
in a distant forest grove,
the tumult falls curiously silent,
yielding to sounds
of ten thousand fleshy things rising.

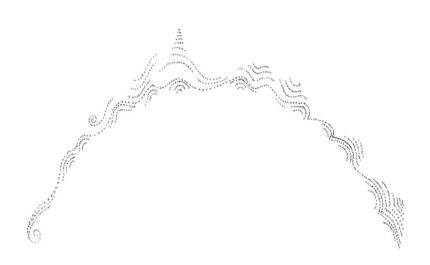

ELECTRON BUTTERFLY

Show me the rocky headland of Hanauma Bay
or the tempestuous tongues
that lick at any shore you wish to name,
and I will call them messengers from the heart of beauty
that sing you down the road, but

raise a finger to your lips,
for what you refrain from expressing too soon
makes you wiser within that space
just beyond the mind.

The electron microscope revealed
the quiescent world of a butterfly wing
as an airy realm of chiffon petals standing in translucent rows,
its iridescent cells leaning forward in architectural precision
flown among by tropical birds.

Pristine beneath the radar of a scheming world,
the secrets of that pearlescent wing
bore testimony to the power of beauty—
an emissary of transcendence
tied to the gravity of the world by sockets and tiny pegs
no less secure in relativity
than steel underpinnings of mighty empires.

The tempestuous tongues and the wing,
fleeting artifacts of some sublime seamless coherence that are,
before they are anything,
sounds before the music is played,
images before they are painted,
movements before their journeys begin—
primordial patterns and potentials
by which
all is woven.

I COULD EAT THIS LAND LIKE SUGAR

I could eat this land like sugar,
sweet-spun piñon pine air
on sage-frosted meadows
with silver aspen arms
stretching to the blue,
laced with tears
of sweet honey rain.

I could eat this land like sugar,
sweet ribbon-rock candy land
layered up cliffs steep
like butter cakes,
hard-baked by sun-spiked
ovens of fire.

I could eat this land like sugar,
sweet kettle-corn cedars
following upland hollows
in lacy patterns of moist green,
murmuring on the wind
like soft wings, waiting
for the ripening time.

UNLESS YOU HEAR THE LAND
Ode to the Petrified Forest

Unless you hear the land,
it lies mostly hidden
among tremors of sparse desert stalks,
naked and unfettered,
whispering a solitary chorus
over silver oceans of sand
and petrified ribbons of rock,
breathing like flesh,
singing on rhythms of wind.

Murmurs of air
playing on shafts of light
ride the strings
and sing with the wind,
their delicate strums on canyon grasses
humming bony spikes of sage,
sounding up the hollows
in riffs of simple joy.

HALEAKALA

At the very loft of the world,
Haleakala holds a luminous prism of air
waiting to be reborn
from the ink-black womb of night.

A flock of white moths
in fluffy hotel robes shiver,
walking ghost-like to the caldera's rim,
picking their way among black boulders
as the predawn sun measures out a slow ascent
through cotton fields of clouds so vast
even Pele holds her volcanic breath.

Suddenly,
a shock of neon green,
blood-bordered,
shoots across the Earth's rim
as a Native daughter steps to the edge
and sings down into the clouds,
sings into the belly of the world,
sings to her ancestors,
sings
to stay
alive.

WIND LIKE A SONG

She holds on tight
to the golden cord,
determined to hang in the wind
like a song
that won't let go.

Someone placed a candle
and a white-painted cross
by the side of the road,
strung with dime-store roses arm to arm,
and scribbled her name with a brush in black.

Now cars fly by,
seldom noticing
that they pierce her silence
with wind
like a song.

DREAMTIME

Down under,
    they sing in dreamtime
        where there is no time,
            no words for time—

no harried countdown times,
    no time-outs,
        timelines,
            no wasted time.

Down under, they say,
    dreamtime hums
        oceans of lullabies
            that blend together,
                some longer,
                    some shorter, and

in luminous moments just right,
    a little hum comes
        to this side of the dream
        and sings you solo
            for a while—

then slips you back
    when it fits the tune,
        to bring you back to home

until the tide sings you out
    to the sea again
        in tones you can hardly hear.

No hurries;
    move slow,
        in rhythms
            that carry you in and out
                and in again—

for the dreamers know
these lullabies rock
a trillion stars
to sleep.

CANADA GEESE

Signs of impending winter
drift down from the north
like a slow drumroll,
bringing musky scents
and the first blush of color.

From the south beckons the magnetic lure of light,
an annual sensuality felt deep within every wing bone—
it's time to go!
And so, as if on cue,
an irresistible urge to follow the sun
overtakes the buttery complacency of summer.

Perhaps it's the wisest among them
who picks up the scent of change
and sends out the call,
or maybe each bird,
with radar sharp and in tune,
rises like a flame
into a gaggle of geese swimming in an ocean of air, and
there they go!—
honking like worn old rubber horns
as their long necks and chin straps stretch forward,
soaring over fields and ponds,
hedgerows and towns
in makeshift arrows,
splicing the air like a knife, and

did you ever feel
the thrill of anything more earnest and driven
than Canada geese
heading south
to their Promised Land?

SNOW MELT

Snow melt,
the shedding of Winter's skin,
an alpine trickle glistening with abandon
like stars—
a tremolo lacing together throaty bass notes
with soprano trills giggling,
riffing off the morning,
gliding, widening—
rushing over rocks; squeezing,
tickling stony gems; and bubbling down
into amber pools
with white-gold patterns dancing on the sand;
shimmering,
receiving the sky; and stretching,
moving into the valley—
    Spring's
        hypnotic
            massage.

BETWEEN HERE AND GONE

Between here and gone,
a command of White-faced Ibis
descend out of lavender
to skid over trees
and drop into the cattail marsh
with the splash of a thousand silky wings.
To welcome this migratory ritual,
bullfrogs throb the air
with sonic density—
an orchestral fortissimo
announcing the arrival
of another spring.

THE GRANDFATHER

The sun eases into the west, spending its gold and staining the clouds crimson as the barefoot boy with long black hair begins his ritual walk. Night hawks sweep the sky along red cliffs that rise like ghost ships from the desert floor. The boy trembles at the thought of meeting his grandfather for the first time. He knows it will not be casual. Arriving after dark, he hesitantly stoops under the low-slung opening of the cave warmed by a fire framed in black. Behind it, his grandfather peers shiny-eyed and solemn. The musky air is ripe with ancestors who had come, one by one, when it was their time. "Sit down, Grandson," the soft raspy voice instructs. The boy settles himself next to the fire. "You have shown yourself, and so you have been chosen. Tonight begins the teaching of sacred stories about our people who came from the stars. Each who hears these stories must carry themselves with dignity, honor, and humility. Gradually, you will become the people's memory." The long, crooked fingers touch a lacing of tooth-like beads around his neck, and he gently murmurs, "One day this will be yours." Firelight makes a crinkled map of the old venerable face and slowly he continues, "Life is a journey, Grandson. It takes a long time to travel from the head to the heart."

Timidly the boy ventures, "What is this road, Grandfather?"

"It is a listening road," the grandfather replies. "Listen to wisdom stirring inside you. Smell the air, touch the skin of the earth, and see with keen questioning eyes. Come to understand how everything fits. Take your time. Wait four days before deciding important things, before speaking your mind. This is our ancient way, Grandson." The grandfather stares into an inner distance, and then he nods. The boy slowly stands. Outside the stars have shifted.

2

BEACH WALK:
THE BAJA COLLECTION

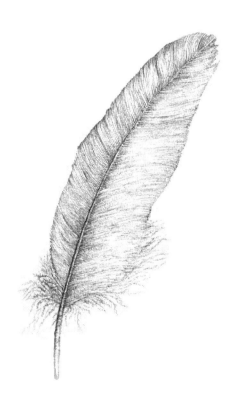

BEACH WALK

It takes time for the sea
to breach inner ramparts,
to tease out the stress
of smaller pursuits
on morning beach walks.

When the walking stops,
tranquility fills inner spaces
as I watch the sea boil,
sending its prancing stalagmites
toward darting sandpipers,
whose choreographed dances
perfectly match
each advancing wave.

The jade-green sea
meets the sky in elusive lines,
where the joining is broken only
by deeply shaded swells
that roll into whitecaps
that slide up the beach and,
by receding,
leave a vast mirror
calling in the sky.

Today, a beached lobster trap
holds a writhing captive
stripped of pincers by scavenger gulls.
It lies helpless with legs skyward
in earnest appeal to no one in particular.

Black dogs prowl the beach
for such morsels in waiting,
as lacy effervescence skitters back to the restless sea,
leaving bubbles like clouds
marking the razor's edge.

PELICAN LINE

Eleven pelicans in a flight line
work the headwind with choreographed precision
wing tips to wave tops,
the leader setting the rhythm
and each in turn picking it up.
She glides and rests,
allowing the wind to play under her long salty wings
as those behind echo the pause.
She pumps her muscular wings again
and the colony picks up the pace,
pushing down hard on the wind—
and over the glimmering coast they sail,
a smooth moving pelican line,
until they d i s a p p e a r

WALKING THE WATERLINE

Walking the waterline
to join the rising sun,
I thread my way among pitted volcanic rocks
sea-carved into narrow bridges,
spotted green with algae
and pocked white with worn embedded shells.
I stop to watch as a slender crane
with yellow eyes pauses,
and we lock eye to eye
  and stay,
  she and I,
  for a while. . .

She fades
when waves steal my attention
with their rhythmic rush and pounding,
and I merge with the sound
  becoming one with the waves
  they and I,
  for a while. . .

In a flash
she spears a fish,
vanishing my reverie,
and I'm pulled from the sound,
  transformed,
  she and I,
  for a while. . .

SEABIRD

Seabird,
you lie on your blue-gray back
with wings outstretched,
trying in vain to navigate the sky,
your yellow eyes glistening inches from the waves,
still soft, supple, newly gone from life.
I stroke your perfect breast
and look closer at your long taffeta feathers,
reaching.

Yesterday,
I asked the sea for a gift
and dared imagine a rare and delicate shell
or marbled rock for the garden.
Instead, here you are, dropped from the sky,
but at such sacrifice!

May I borrow your feathers
to make a fan for smudging sweet grass and sage
so that, in some distant kind of way,
you will fly?

LOW TIDE

Peering into pockets of seawater
closely held by craggy cavern walls,
I discover petite empty shells
shaped like unicorn horns
white, open, and scattered.

Captive minnows
dart among these shadowed walls,
seeking cover as each sea rush
assails them, dashed and buffeted,
within their minikin water pools.

Snails with shells perched like burden baskets
crawl over the glittering moonscape terrain,
tracing delicate serpentine lines that loop and twist,
forming dance maps in slow motion—
lacy etchings
that take my breath
away.

SHELL FRAGMENTS

Shell fragments,
nestled in beach rows left by receding tides,
beckon.

Slowly,
I sift and sort each bony gem,
choosing only ones with tiny holes
made from grinding, restless waves.

I taste one.
It's salty from the sea.
This is my gold today
as I imagine a necklace
strung thick
with shell fragments.

WATCH WHAT'S HAPPENING NOW!

Walking the beach,
I whisper to myself,
watch the energy.
I am this, and this is me.
Watch what's happening
now!

Illusive mood shadows
parade through my mind,
momentary,
ephemeral—
be open,
be aware,
be here!

I wonder to myself,
are mood shadows
so very different from sun shadows
floating across a landscape,
changing the shape of things
I believe I see?
Just watch,
watch what's happening
now!

3

PROMISE OF FULLNESS

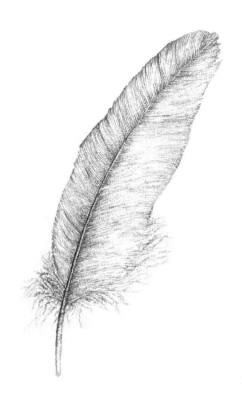

HOW CAN I SAY I LOVE YOU?

How can I say
I love you
when you are not a thing,
nor is love?

Oh, indefinable, diaphanous love,
we try in vain to hold it in our hands
like water, but
back to you.

You who are more like the velvet pulse
of a living wing,
a process, mysterious, elusive,

that I observe
still unfolding
within the circle of my heart.
I see you now

as juicy movement,
a shimmering light
living just beneath the mask,
beautiful,
ultimately unknowable,

an incandescence
of something grander
breathing on the other side—

a song shivering along a string,
a wave moving through space,
moving through my skin,
moving me to feel lovingly
that you are.

WENDY'S GREENHOUSE

Wendy's greenhouse fills a corner of the old seasoned yard
standing like a ghostly sentinel over living remains of two generations.
She tends the vintage geraniums
growing among the moth orchids and angel wing begonias,
blooming to spurn a doyen's demise.

Her grandmother Berta's "Charlie Plant"
lives beside Aunt Evalee's euphorbic legacy—
a quirky collection with exotic flowers.
The succulent haworthia from Africa lives mostly under soil,
its translucent leaves allowing in the light,
and she speaks of the adenium, astrophyton, and pachypodiums
who jostle for space in their earthen homes like their names compete
for space on the tongue.

Wendy's contributions are bulbous clay planters
with indentations made from antique rings she inherited,
hand forged keys she bought in Venice,
and shark bones she collected on beaches in Mexico.
She presses each treasure into soft fleshy clay,
making the surfaces come alive
like Berta and Evalee in the blossom of their time.

With an enigmatic smile and gentle hands,
Wendy notices each nuance of growth and decay—
pruning stems and widening root spaces
with an unspoken kind of love
that keeps the conversation going.

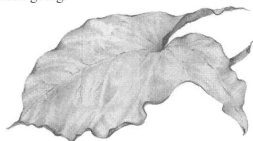

VALENTINE'S DAY ON THE SURGICAL WARD

10:00 p.m.
and a steady hiss escapes
from the battle-gray serpentine ducts,
filtering out microbial invaders
slithering down white polished hallways.
If you think about what lurks,
the future might exhale into your face
and snuff out the sun.

His breath rolls out in thin ribbons,
causing colors to curl through the darkness,
turning their delicacy
into a warning.

Down the hall,
nurses disappear into pockets of night and pits of pain—
witness to disappointment and shame-filled stories,
the complex amalgam of suffering.

On this particular Valentine's Day,
Julie shakes her high-perched ponytail,
revealing that even a veteran army nurse
can be surprised by what human ingenuity
performs as love.

Tonight,
a three-quarter moon hangs over this restless labyrinth
filled with lives making right-angle turns
in vulnerable bodies struggling to remember
when love was new
and bore no scars.

TELL YOUR MOTHER

I
The veil can be thin at the edges
when most of the living is done.
Take the frail man in blue flannel pajamas,
a whisper of what he was,
holding to the world
with its clanging unhinged.

II
Calendar dates come and go,
flashing on screens with abandon
while stiff-legged automatons track, count, and tick off time,
shouting out the order of things
in cacophonous absolutes and protocols
layering up a thick veneer,
driven by quarrelsome, firmly ensconced monkey-judges,
who thrash about behind grandiose lock-down doors
while those with any remaining flesh
struggle to shrink from the din.

III
The Master Muse hustles in silent rhythm,
diligent, almost breathless,
gathering obscure connections
like rose petals scattered by a summer storm,
stitching them together into glorious raiment
laced with jewel tones.
He works in the dark of night,
trimming here, stitching there in stooped labors of love
so the morning will be greeted with the beauty of the work.

IV
Words tumble out in disarrayed,
startling combinations.
"We are cantilevers of light!" he blurts,
and who is to know if some quantum wisdom is at play?

V

The family often props up the old man in the living room,
who sits in a distant kind of joining.
When suddenly he slumps over, gray as rain,
one son shouts to the other, *"Call nine-one-one!"*
The father, suddenly clear,
speaks in a way not heard in years,
"I'm OK.
Don't call nine-one-one.
I'm leaving now.
Tell your mother
I love her."

YOU TOOK ME AS I AM

You took me as I am
with no hesitation,
like the simple honesty of rain.
I imagine you remember.

There were birds at sunrise, and
drawn to the sound,
I quietly came.

It was you I saw
emerging from the ether.
Our eyes met again,
and this time it was more than love—

it was a solidarity,
an arising
incalculably
sweet.

THESE DAYS WITH YOU

Autumn rolls into the close of summer
with golds and russets washing over the tattered edges
that only certain endings know.

Our coffee pot comes on more quickly now,
the robes and slippers too,
as spokes of early light overtake more slowly
the recesses of night.

The gray of winter arrives hesitantly,
every portion and limb wary to succumb to dormancy,
yet ready, in some oblique kind of way,
to enter the annual introspection
like Cro-Magnon to his ritual cave.

Daffodils are gone to dust,
the bougainvillea to faded parchment.
Craggy nests with bounty flown
loosen from their branches,
and shadows come to life
in the candlelight of night.

You seem more quiet now,
perhaps thinking over what has gone before—
the things completed and still left to do,
the perceived imperfections and little regrets,
the rapid passing and pleasures too.

Sometimes on a long drive
or over breakfast, like today,
the marrow of our lives turns transparent,
and I see it isn't just happenstance
that the seasons have rolled one into the other
swelling rhythms that say,
I'm glad I've spent these days with you.

SKIN

Born of a deeper substance
than a fleshy cover
can provide
stark
angular bones,

a curious fullness
lies beneath
the moist,
speckled
satin of your skin

as rocks
cloaked in mossy blankets
hold deeper mysteries
than velvet covers
can conceal.

PROMISE OF FULLNESS

There's a silver sliver
of a moon
over us tonight.

Held in its cup
is the gossamer promise
of fullness.

4

ANOTHER ROOT AND STEM

ANOTHER ROOT AND STEM

The spring garden
spills into summer with pillars of color—
the penstemon pinks and marigold yellows,
the lime of the aloe and lavender of the blue hill salvia.

A lone zucchini bears mostly male flowers this year,
and few bees come,
so the elephant-eared plant seems bereft,
its fleshy saffron trumpets fading quickly
as if they acknowledge defeat
even before the sun peers above the top of the wall.
I go early to the garden with feathery brush in hand,
hoping to coax a reticent blossom into fruiting,
if one might show its silky face.

The mullein, transplanted from high in the canyon,
adapts quickly, opening her furry wings in a wide rosette
as if possessed of hinges, but not this morning.
She folds inward as if afraid
of the killer falcon who storms the yard,
causing the air to chill
and the doves and sparrows
to shiver in the leaves.

This spring we painted the garden wall the color of persimmons
and added the golden breath of Quetzalcoatl
that spreads east and west in broad spirals from the purple gate.
Perhaps he, in his wisdom, might return the bees.

My friend speaks of her deepening relationship with surrender,
and I know it to be mine as well,
how it sometimes feels too much like succumbing.
We agree, that over time,
we yield to what is and ripen,
allowing summers to grow us forward
and winters to give us pause—

etching lines on our faces,
leaving messages that,
in spite of all the departing,
we birth another root and stem.

AUTUMN BUTTERFLY

Supple leaves of summer give way and stiffen into autumn,
calling ephemeral sky dwellers to the ground.
This one with folded wings,
her black legs skinny as carpet threads,
lace together, stilled.

Iridescent black and blazing nuggets of gold
played the skies in which her delicacy flew
with pulse and swing and dip and dart
through summer's luminous air.

For a short time,
a filigree of transcendence
flew like a secret wish beneath her wings,
altering the winds in China
and compelling her parchment flesh
to seek buttery pollen cups
and swell her kind in chambered lanterns of green.

She never promised she could stay—
nor can I, nor can you,
given the fleeting flesh we wear
that rusts and quakes
and falls to this garden ground—
but not before our time in spring
when rushes come to fill our wings
and pierce our tiny veils with light.

FOUR SEASONS TICKING DOWN

Four seasons
ticking down,
closing out
to a few calculated days that,
added to the rest and taken as a whole,
swell to a lifetime
seen best at the back end.

We cast our colors in myopic array,
juxtaposing fears and dreams
in a ragtag mix,
mostly imagining ourselves a singular digit
as if the wave does not belong to the sea.

At New Year's tentative cusp,
a new page is already partly written
as we proceed to the next ephemeral spring,
adding imperceptibly as we go
to the structure of the whole,
behaving mostly
as if our lives
don't depend on it.

WHAT BETTER TIME THAN WINTER

What better time than winter
to strip down
to the bare wood
and tender skin,

to blow the dust
off self-deception and the obsolete,
to shed the little titles and positions,
to let the heartwood sing—
and where will I take
this naked self?

The winter sun swings low,
and lingering darkness crowds the morning.
I vow, in this stillness,
to forage in the dimness,
to watch the self-reemerge
so the snow,
when it melts,
can soak to the heartwood—
to sing it open,
to sing it true.

COME WINTER

Winter leaves,
dry, hump-backed, and folded,
lie in random heaps
beneath the molted chinaberry
with its long skinny stems yellowing
and sinking in reluctant demise
to the garden's breast.

Sparrows gather to chitter
within the tangle of the sparse winter bush,
then dart like fish
to the frigid ground in skittish schools,
pummeling spare morsels
that drum the morning air.

When traffic throbs
like rushing water,
and sirens shriek
in calamitous push,
I turn to mesquite flour pancakes
flush with sunflower seed meal
and topped with honey butter,
which work a simple solace
come winter.

THE ALOE

I come to watch the spring garden come alive
and the old pair of ring-necked doves dive in for seed.
I thank my friend dying with grace
with Buddha on her lips,
as I breathe perfume from the gardenias
and witness the sun perched on neon blue lobelia.
Strawberries are waiting,
the basil, dill, and rosemary too.
French marigolds are shouting saffron,
and pomegranates are swelling to perfection
next to the Aloe—
the Aloe,
the Aloe,
a chorus in almighty
OM.

HOW HAPPY CAN HAPPY BE

How happy can happy be, I wonder,
as I slowly walk the morning garden under a precocious spring
ripe with the scent of orange blossoms.

Along the narrow path laced with mimosa and redbud branches,
shafts of aboriginal light fall on daffodils just opened
and newly potted geraniums singing radiance to the birds
giving voice to the aliveness of it all.

Overcome with pleasure,
I wonder if two such gardens
could swell my happiness to twice as much.
Would it be a matter of exponentials—
an alchemy of happiness
grown in proportion
to the number of gardens I could walk?

But maybe happiness gets so full
it can't hold anymore,
like a pitcher when it reaches capacity,
or are such constraints reserved
only for things we can touch,
preserving the freedom to soar
toward things our tiny fingers
cannot reach?

FLEETING CLOTH OF THE WORLD

Breeze whispers
park dry leaves in spirals along the ground,
gathering in loose clutches and subtle patterns
as if elves with tiny brooms
spent the night swirling and skidding them
in a great autumn waltz.

The early sun edges up into the sky
like a tendril of flesh deep in the heart of spring,
pushing until it bursts open the night
reclaiming the world.

Inky shadows transform
into gold and scarlet,
and birds on spare chilly branches
sing to the sacredness of dawn,
their ardent voices weaving
the fleeting cloth
of the world.

LEAVES AND FEATHERS

Leaves and feathers
form like rivers ripe with tributaries and
highways linked with side roads,
embellishing the edges
of what we are—

shaping for a time
our bodies
and then,
at the apogee of our fullness,
let go
into the autumn molt

to fade and fall
from air to earth,
making space
for new leaf buds and feather quills
in perpetual plays
of sun
and shade.

HEAT SOUNDS

Heat sounds,
    red-spiked and groaning,
        sear the skin and lean in close, pounding—

a jackhammer kind of heat
    that begins in the morning
        and ascends to high afternoon
            with hot winds swelling
                and breezes spending themselves
                    in dry sandy washes.

Raspy skinny limbs of chaparral
    shrink from the inferno
        that moves in shimmering waves,
            corkscrewing through the air in ropes of fire.

From secret places,
    ravens shriek to relentless suns
        that scorch jojoba gripping leaves bereft of water
        and cry to manzanita splayed open,
            gasping for monsoons
                still a dream in waiting.

At last, when rains come,
    breezes swell with intoxicating perfume
        as the inferno succumbs to soft white sheets,
            blue under a sterling moon—
                undulating with succulence
                    and orange blossom wine.

CUTTING PEACHES

Cutting peaches,
juice dripping,
slipping through fingers
like luminous nectar from unseen gods
falling from plump tender orbs
dressed in blazing yellows and russet reds
like sunsets
with meat
impossibly gold.

A sweet fruity fragrance
shoots through the air
in waves of manna
as skins peel away in soft velvety shards
after the quick rolling boil.

The knife finds the subtle valley at the stem end,
inviting a slit to the heart seed
the color of blood,
revealing veins rooted in sumptuous flesh so full
they pulse with summers
that end in hot peach pies
with flaky crusts
and smiles wrapped wide
in whipped cream dreams.

Peeling,
cutting,
working the fruit in rhythm to its natural inclinations,
the quintessential fruit becomes a sage
held shining
in the hand.

UNČÍ MAKĤÁ*

Feel the breeze of Unčí Makĥá on your face,
and smell Her fragrance of cedar and sage in the air;
touch Her skin of stone, petal, and feather,
and hear Her rustling tree pods and birds at sunrise.

Feel how She relieves your thirst with her waters
and invites you to rest on velvet carpets of moss
when you are tired and need to dream.

When She is in spring, feel refreshed by Her playfulness;
when She is in summer, feel Her strength.
When She is in autumn, feel compelled to prepare and store away;
when She is in winter, feel drawn into reflection and rest.

By Her rhythms we pace our days;
by Her sky we navigate our way.
From Her clouds we make poetry,
and from Her chill we draw ourselves together.
By Her warmth we know love;
from Her caverns we are born into light, and
when it is time,
to Her
we return.

*A Lakota term of address for the earth and its powers.
Literal meaning: Grandmother Earth. Used in prayers and
ceremonies.

OMÉ TÉOTL*

"Omé Téotl,"
the great elder said, as we parted,
his long black hair in a thick braid,
a wide woven cummerbund bound at his waist.
"Omé Téotl," Tlakaelel repeated.
His solid voice echoed in my bones
long after his right arm crossed over his chest
with its fist resting on his heart
and his left arm and fist crossed to the right.
To impart its meaning,
the gesture had to be carefully constructed
so to create a narrow space between the arms—
a symbol perhaps as old as Teotihuacan itself.
This space between opposites
is profound and succulent,
"like a battery," he said,
a space before color, shape, or sound,
before the ripening into form,
a birthing place giving life—
clear, open, and receptive.

I will meet you there.

*oh may tay oatl

49

5

CLIMB THE HIGH STAIRS

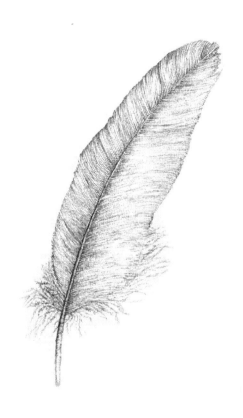

CLIMB THE HIGH STAIRS

Come,
climb the highest stairs,
and cast the fetters off
while there is still time, this time.
Have we an idea
how long this has waited?

The cycle is wide,
circling beyond deep spaces of blue,
and this house,
with windows scratched
and doors slanting off their hinges,
stands by.

Often now it seems incomplete
with rooms still in the making,
as we who live here
slowly work the edges outward
and from rough and stained
to a kind of smooth.

The old place has a low little door
to the long haul
that opens to the air at the end,
which moves within this wideness now
that always was—
and so we see,
sometimes.

SMALL BIRD FLEDGES

Small bird fledges,
winging through the blue-green flesh of spring,
she not a song
but a singing,
the season not a spring
but a springing—
her maiden flight
a translucent lift
into the world of wind—
a living,
silent,
floating
dream.

We widen our arms at last
to the unfolding,
we not a breath
but a breathing,
we not a ripple
but a rippling—
trepidations on ephemeral
earth-bound journeys
through realms of color
into the silent opening
of our transcendent
winging.

INNOMINATE RIVER

Innominate River,
you flow with no partialities or partitions,
carrying every cause and condition,
but I see only what moves beside me:
a loss, a circumstance, a petty annoyance,
and then it passes,
overtaken by another set of elations and trivialities,
each seeming to rise as if in isolation,
disconnected from the rest.

I course through your watery web
feeling your fullness and complexity,
your wild, raucous vitality and,
in the most quiet of moments,
sense your paradoxical, generative emptiness.
It is then I think to myself,
loosen the grip,
preferences are only relevant in the moment,
and all that is not open and generous is mischief!

And I imagine, when all numbers are run
and all hypotheses spent,
it will be found that your unifying factor
is the quantum
equivalent
of love.

BALANCE

In the teeter and shift,
an alchemical language of balance reigns,
whose predictions are futile
regarding how things might play—

the way he or she (or it)
might proceed or turn and,
leaning into the dance,
so too the stars,
some falling,
some swelling into unions—

the icicle in winter becomes the cloud in spring,
the autumn leaf becomes the soil of summer—
dissolving,
pivoting,
reeling,
rising.

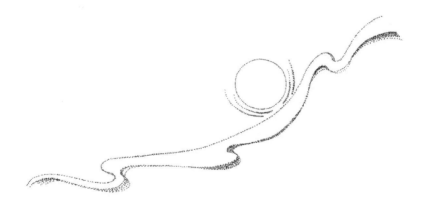

MANTIS RELIGIOSA

From autumn air
drops a super-sized praying mantis, green as grass,
who lands on my white breakfast plate, waking me up
as all such things do that arrive by surprise—
messengers of some magnificent whole,
when the moment is right.

Her majesty
strolls leisurely through the scrambled eggs and salsa
with arms outstretched and empty, like mine.
I slip away for a solitary time,
skipping down the dirt road
moistened with midnight rain.

WHERE DO WE BIRDS FLY

Where do we birds fly
but up into the great silence
that spins the cosmic dust,
returning
to where we began
by grace
of an inner compass,
unfolding
despite the bargaining
that our days be different than they are,
lengthened or shortened, and
who can say
when the concourse has cleared
and the heart made ready
for the great sojourn forward
where there is no arriving
at transcendent ethers
already
come.

AND THEN, MY LOVE

The prayer is just air until you say it,
    the heart is mute until you sing it,
        the ceremony is dormant until you do it, so

bend slowly at the knees,
    down. . .down,
        until the bones beneath your flesh
            blend with the russet of her succulent skin
                flushed and alive and

merge with her crystal rock body,
    deeper. . .deeper,
        until her scented wind-carved canyons
            freeze with ice and melt wild with rain,
                thundering you up to the rushing, and then

the eagle will play the wind in liquid song,
    skyward. . .skyward,
        as you set upon the hero's journey
            singing praises to the sun

as watching ones
    stretch you jubilant
        to the indivisible divinity of blue,
            and then, my love,
                you fly.

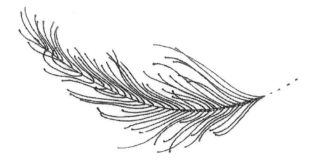

SILENT REMNANTS

In our time,
there were few shadows
we did not wear
and few times we did not need the strength
of silent remnants who walked before us
until, at last,
we found our way toward wisdom
that sustained our earthly veils.

It is your time now,
so take our breath
and breathe it full
with strength that cups the winter moons
and ripples silver new spring rains
until, at last,
you find our soft embrace
within the home of your own arms.

Take our silent drumming now
and pulse it full,
encircling your torn fragments
until, at last,
they mend with sounds
that soar you up on wings
above the tempest
of your life.

In the valley of our footsteps,
let your lips whisper the old tones
of our ancient remnants
that suggest possibilities
you've not dared ask of your life
until, at last,
you find your way
and can call them
your own.

SOLSTICE CANDLE FLAME

Solstice candle flame,
remnant of First Light,
daughter of dancing suns,
you flicker with primordial fire.

Sister of the Wellspring,
imbue with peace this quiet place,
soften our ragged edges,
and beckon to your light
those who suffer and are lost.

Prancing flame,
kin to all who labor to live,
breathe into us the radiance of your fire
so we will remember
the light from which we come.

May this Day of Turning renew us in midwinter
so spring will find in us a fertile field,
where kindly things can thrive, multiply,
and walk with generosity!

ONCE WE WERE BIRDS

Once we were birds
  with hollow bones
    that drew up incense
      from some finer kind of ether
        than our wings could fly, yet
          still we flew and still we fly
          by the dreams in our veins,
        pulsing with color,
      coursing us forward
    we know not to where,
  blind but for hope, deaf
but for the distant ringing.

SHARDS

What object
or circumstance,
when finished,
is not a shard—
testament to a process
exquisite or tragic,
immense or miniscule
like love when it is done
or a summer rose when it has faded.

And so it is,
for now,
that we are—
gossamer threads
woven by the grand parade,
fleeting in our outcropping
and precious because of it.

In this ephemeral moment
within which all things arise and are gone,
what matters most is that we love enough
to swell our essence into the time and space we share,
reflecting the shining
of the who
that we are.

CANTILEVERS OF LIGHT

What are we,
really,
but fragile, tenuous
tendrils of grass
wafting in and out of this breezy world,
our small domains made for a while
of vaulted joy,
harbors of comfort, and
pits of fire—
dreaming the impossible,
doing the unimaginable,
too often blind to save ourselves, and yet
in our finest hours,
we transcend
into cantilevers of light.

TO ENTER THIS IMMENSITY

Among a thicket of leaves and blossoms, the air is alive
as it weaves between each stem and airborne root.
Lushness fills the pregnant space with hypnotic peace,
moving through my bones,
meeting each breath as though, a moment before,
I had been asleep.

In my absence,
humility of movement has opened a blossom,
lengthened a stem, and readied an herb for an omelet.

Stillness encourages a certain wisdom that passes unnoticed
unless greeted with a quietude
relinquished of preference or opinion
about the way things ought to be.

The secret language spoken here
knows no word for perfection or imperfection—
each leaf and flower confirming
that something larger unfolds.

Am I small enough
to enter this immensity?

RAVEN SONG

Just before the blinding light of Essence
burst open the clenched fist of darkness,
emptiness waited in vast potential, and
as darkness reached its apogee,
Raven sang her wake-up song.

It began as a shiver
and then rushed forth
in sparkling silver, stirring sounds
that formed a vortex with no edge,
moving and swirling in boundless winds
that poured out perfect rhythms
of expanding light, and

into this awakening,
Essence breathed,
creating illusions of in and out,
black and white,
now and then,
here and there,
and the great jewel of paradox was born.
Everywhere was nowhere,
and each arising became a diamond speck
amid the seamless heart
of the whole.

In dreamtime,
Raven's song rises
to sing the great nameless cycles—
where endings are the set points of beginnings,
where the call of demise
transforms our rare and precious journeys
back to spring.

TEA CEREMONY

Harmony,
respect,
purity, and
tranquility
begin on this quiet Sunday afternoon
under a monsoon-seasoned sky just off the garden,
as water boils in a song, and
macha is sifted and piled high like Mt. Fuji rising
in the black-lacquered natsume.

Delicate crowns of pink and orange lantana
tilt gracefully in the humble vase,
and incense sends a languid trail
that shivers slightly,
then pivots sideways
and rights itself again,
revealing invisible currents
meandering skyward,
leaving spicy traces
of woody quiet places.

Steaming water
sends clouds into waiting tea bowls
with red silk fukusa
unfurling,
folding,
in slow legato—
a precisely paced
choreographed dance
of chawan,
chasen,
chakin, and chashaku
in genteel motions
echoing the ancient ritual, tethered to now,
in plays of clay, water, silk, and tea.

The mind settles and opens
like a dry brittle leaf
soaked and softened by gentle rain,
and ears attune to hypnotic swells
of breezes threading through pine boughs
and water bubbling over pebbles in spring.

When time unfolds just right,
macha greets the tongue like an anam cara,
knocking three times at the door and,
under the spell,
calms and graces the space,
then slips discreetly away
through the low and narrow door,
leaving fragrance
in the air.

A WOMAN SLIPS INTO THE FOREST

Curious and weary of the world,
a woman slips into the forest
to walk, listen, and sit by streams.
For two years she sleeps in a simple one-room cabin,
entering the wilderness each day
to witness its primeval fullness.

She settles into contours of boulders
that mirror her own and peers
into each unfurling thing
to explore its evolving story.

She observes stems and succulent blades of grass
becoming pillars for tiny beings
who clamber up to warm in the sun
and suck their heart of sweetness.

She spies on secret missions
to find treasures for winter lodges
and sees how each small participant
contributes, in miniscule ways,
to a spiraling crescendo of complexity.

She watches flowers bloom and fade
according to their mandate
and sees each seductive blossom birth the next
to ignite responses far beyond its ephemeral self.

She senses the presence of faceless intermediaries
who form networks extending to the stars,
had we the eyes to see.

WHAT IF THE PEARLY MOON

What if the pearly moon
shares a communal thread with blades of grass in spring
and crickets clambering up willowy stems in summer,
with you in your autumn
and me in my winter?

What if laughter is kin to the moon,
whelk to the heart of the mountain,
and stars to leaves on the trees?

What if an essence weaves itself so completely
within and between every stripe and color,
penetrating the collective of things so seamlessly,
that we are rendered blind to see?

What if hills and valleys of this fertile thread
so weave and move within the interior of things
that we are complete as we are
and perfect in this moment,
even in the face of the fiercest wind
we perceive pains and divides us—

and if we perceived this truth,
how might we move forward
through this fragile, shining world?

WHY THE BUFFALO CRIES

The buffalo cries
long mournful bellows
that grab us by the gut
and shake us till we wake
from our languid sleep,
to take the webbing
from our eyes,
eyes drenched too long in darkness—

darkness from the illusion
that things are as we think them to be
or hope that they are,
like love or the next vacation,
what the child will grow to be
(or not to be),
and, for that matter, the past,
the past we've so constricted—

constricted in, oh, such holy nights,
but these were not for naught.
We wept until darkness saturated
and filled us until we could take no more—
filled us until our bodies bent
and our heads bowed to touch the earth,
and then we wept again,
wept though we knew not why—

why the evening star
follows the sunset,
why the sun follows the night,
why the resurrection follows the fall.
Such things are so constructed—

constructed as we'd hoped they were not,
for there's nothing to grasp
but gossamer threads

congealing here, then there
in fleeting unions,
binding and loosening,
floating deceivingly free
with nothing forever committed,
nothing coming from everything,
everything absorbed into nothing—
only benevolent, terrifying,
magnificent, numbing,
endlessly rumbling change—

change never ending?
Then why does it matter what we do
if what we do is changed
and what is changed
disappears—

disappears?
Ah, but for gossamer threads
would our fate be sealed,
for they seem to have no agenda,
and nothing other to do
than align with images, perhaps,
of something, somewhere—

somewhere in the beginning
and in each new day,
there breathes a catalyst
that spins and weaves its energy,
causing planets to be drawn from dust
and light to be spun from darkness
like iron fillings pulled into patterns.

Could there possibly be a magnet?

PRIMORDIAL SOUND

Primordial
sound,
slow and resonant,
crests and falls
with undulations
of luminous color
permeating the dark,
making distinct the nameless,
jettisoning the great obscurities
that merge and mix their textured tones
in majestic unions
to birth the waters
that wash the fields
with green and flowered spectacles,
cascading into ever finer details
that burrow into the recesses
of the receptive
hungry heart.

IF YOU CLIMB HIGH ENOUGH

if you climb high enough
all things are analogous
one thing appearing no larger or smaller than the next
no particle of us better than another
we
no less
and no more
than the stars

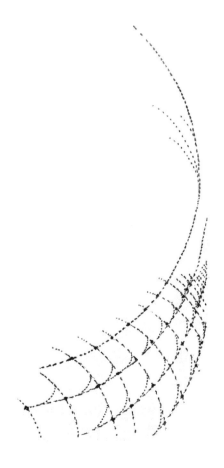

CYSTALLINE

crystalline quanta
      in crystalline bodies
            in crystalline worlds
                  in crystalline universes
endlessly dancing
      form to form
            gliding
                  sliding
shifting
      shining

NO SUCH THING

stasis   no such thing
        temporal   mercurial   fixation is false
            morning glories   fleeting
                birds of paradise   winging
                    moonflowers   floating
                        blossoms of nightshades   waning

autumn falling   spring rising
        nano relevancies   no sense judging what is changing
            moving forward   and forgiving
                breathing in   breathing out

inside   outside   rivers transforming
        all   ways reconstructing
            new eyes   fresh chances
                calla lilies   white   for now
                    no time   for indifference

you   me
        opening
            closing
                coming
                    going

did you
        see it
            while it
                lived?

WHAT IS THIS WIND

What is this wind
singing us into being,
living beneath our stories
with no beginning,
no once upon a time,
no ending with amen?

What is this wind
but the whispering Muse
breathing us alive,
stirring the chi
and coursing us forward
though mostly we have forgotten?

What is this wind
moving within the ebony-eyed raven,
compelling her to proclaim
her truth at first light?

What is this wind
living in our bones,
painting our canvas,
and weaving our poems like incense
to dream us—
giving us birth and setting us free,
winging through the dross
leaving feathers
on our doorstep?

WHO CAN KNOW?

My grandmother, at ninety-three, said to my mother,
"Rudy, it all goes so fast. "

Does the illusion of time count for something—
all the hours and years
that seem to vanish while on the run?

Perhaps there is an energetic aftertaste
that gathers at the edges—
an essence that collects along our way—and
how long it lingers,
who can know?

?

?
imply
might this
possibilities
what unconsidered
might we flower and
come to believe in, how
imaginary solidarities we have
and if we were able to rise above our
their confines into the fluency of the open air,
particles rising like tendrils of flame, stretching from
dissipated upward, escaping the bondage of gravity, their
What if the mountains, instead of decaying downward into valleys,

Please begin here

ONCE WE WERE TRAPPED

Once
we were trapped
believing the earth was flat.

Now we are trapped
believing the earth is round.

—Tim Ballingham

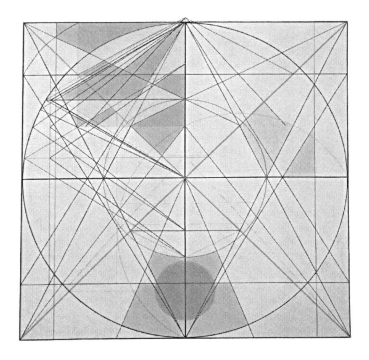

6

EVEN THE OCEAN
HAS A FLOOR

I CLOSE THE STEELY DOOR

I close the steely door
on this unsettled world
to watch the morning sun shout gold
through my window filled with clouds of pink fleshy orchids
whose emerald airborne roots
reach like fingers for the mystery
that sings this quintessential world.

A midwinter fly
presses her iridescent belly to the glass
toward the mimosa tree who waits naked in the yard.
She draws sun-soaked legs across each other like violin bows
rehearsing for the distant spring,
as if she will live to get there.

I disappear into the warm black sand
within the upturned hourglass on the sill,
watching the long steady drumroll
into the crystal abyss below,
imagining the grains came
from ebony beaches of Maui's eastern end,
pummeled by the blue Pacific hurling its might
against volcanic cliffs and caverns
we once explored.

Each grain succumbs to the slowly twisting hollow
that presses through the narrow
like a glistening sun bursting into the pulsing mound below,
whose shifting slopes rise and fall,
and rise again,
like a diamond Phoenix until,
at last,
the stream
is spent.

THE SCREAM
(Ode to Edvard Munch)

The
scream
can go unnoticed
for nearly a lifetime until it hits the ceiling and
bounces down like an engorged raindrop falling from lofty heights,
making a splash like
brittle bits of
broken
glass.

DREAM FRAGMENTS

Dream
fragments,
like dust balls,
skitter to corners
from breezes of current affairs
lingering unnoticed until
shards of memory
make sleepwalkers
of our living
breathing
daylight.

NOVEMBER DREAM

I forgot to tend the amber sand
held within the glass box,
so where once there were ants
burrowing and lining their nests,
now a terrible stillness falls.
I should have placed a leafy twig for them to chew,
a sugary plant for them to harvest,
a little cup of water—
but I'd never had an ant garden
and am bereft, wondering
what I've left
untended.

YOU CAN SWEEP THE FLOOR

You can sweep the floor
and whitewash the walls
only so many times
before you see trees out there,
large fruit-filled ones—
the toothsome and the honeyed.
When loneliness fell so hard and roared,
the road turned inside out,
and now a grace not of my own
pulls me to the door.

ONCE THE WORLD

Once
the world held itself open
(at least that's what it seemed),
and we imagined we could enter it
from just about anywhere, wide-eyed,
adding to the succulent mix.

Long arms held candles against the dark,
illuminating great complexities
and calming the shivers
as we stepped into the great churn.

Probing and questioning,
we felt the world supportive,
like shining water
beneath our young, teetering boats.

Dreams and intuition were our allies
and anticipation the grand palette
on which our colors floated and thrived
as we navigated unfamiliar places.

Fledged and free, we sailed,
believing something splendid would come—
believing the heart of the world
was good.

SERPENT AND SATIN PILLOW

On the cusp of the turning year,
Serpent, patient and relentless,
slips through the back door
under a new moon.

It circles and tightens,
casting its shadow, landing,
stealthily shedding
it's sixtieth skin.

Luminous,
Satin Pillow sits
caught mostly unaware,
living
the timeless
dream.

OLD BEULAH'S SPRING

Firemen broke down the door, and
EMTs took old Beulah away—
just broke down the door and took her away.
Few others had ever gone to that door.

Our redbud tree is blooming now,
and the air is fresh and fragrant.
Color is beginning to show on the lilac bush.

Old Beulah is chalk white;
her dry mouth opens like a cry.
We gently touch her hand,
hoping she knows someone's here.

We're hungry for spring and
walk along the nursery aisles,
choosing sweet alyssum and pink begonias.

Above unseeing eyes,
her brow is furrowed, and her arms jerk
as though trying to push something fearsome away.

We discuss where we'll place each plant in our yard.
Will we use the large terracotta pots
or the ones with bright blue glazes,
and where will we plant the vegetable garden this year?

The teddy bear from old Beulah's bedroom looks lonely,
nestled in her vacant arms.
The nurse suggests we take her reading glasses away.

A shiny red barbeque leaves the garden store
in a bright yellow pickup, blaring Dolly Parton.
Last night, a mockingbird began its mating song
in old Beulah's backyard.

We empty her refrigerator,
turn off the light,
and take old Beulah's trash away.

EVEN THE OCEAN HAS A FLOOR

"Even the ocean has a floor," she murmured
in our last moments together.
She put down her wings,
pale with surrender,
into the hollow of her pillow,
stripped of pretense
in those waning hours.

"You've been the greatest love of my life,
beautiful, beautiful, beautiful," she whispered.
Her eyes took in the early light
as her crooked fingers stroked my hand lying on her chest.
The immensity of those words
wove their way
into the marrow of me.

The simple room held us in those naked hours
as prophetic words poured from the heart of her,
made possible by every semblance of dignity stripped—
the diaper, the ungainly man's striped shirt of unknown origin
delivered in haste from the laundry department.
None of it mattered except her transcendent clarity.

"I'll come again, I promise," I said.
"No, no, no," she gently admonished,
her still-graceful fingers stroking the air,
"we must not make promises we cannot keep.
Lie down, take a nap," she suggested as her eyes closed,
and I knew she sought comfort,
thinking we would sleep together for a time.

I tidied up the spare little room,
leaving my chair next to her bed,
then slipped reluctantly away,
knowing she was too wise
to say good-bye.

TO THE MUSIC

A drop swells on the faucet's rim,
a crystal slowly gathering itself,
filling like a day and
disappearing like the rest.

Her stiff fingers curl into themselves,
bird-like,
with brown patches on her hands like late winter fields.
My soothing voice moves through her
as tears fill her hollows,
and she whispers, "I love you too, sweetheart."

Her face barely reflects who she was—
a great beauty and fierce arbiter of discernment,
who sought to drink life through a silver straw,
hoping for a sweet sip of honey.

Leaving with a delicacy such times imply,
I vow to bring the secret part of her that loves
to the oceans,
to the gardens,
to the music.

MY FATHER'S VIOLIN

My grandfather
gave my father
his violin made in Austria,
it was told.
At ninety-four, he still loves this violin,
this shapely ancestral shard,
this sculpted belly that sings.
My father's narrowing shoulders
cradle the amber-colored gem
as he tucks it between chin
and thinning collarbone,
holding the old unruly bow
like the long, quivering wing
of some magnificent bird.
He plays a legacy of reels, hornpipes, and strathspeys,
disappearing into an expanse of thought
only music is clever enough to convey—
the cadence of steps up mountains he climbed,
the ski tracks etched on snow-feathered slopes,
the rhythm of paddles on white rivers he rushed
as he teased the roar and the razor's edge,
playing the wild blue pulse
and sweet succulence
of this world.

OLD MAN RIVER

The great silver belly descends from freedom onto the hot tarmac, rolling to a stop. Her mind snaps back in a whiplashed time warp, memories unhinged. Too soon, she stands at the old iron-clad door with musty baggage in tow, feeling caught in the crossfire between recollections and new resolutions. She descends steep stairs to the basement with its ghosts and tilted photographs. Nothing has changed. The place remains filled with dog-eared scores extolling the life of Old Man River with his head still high, absent of truths he might never know.

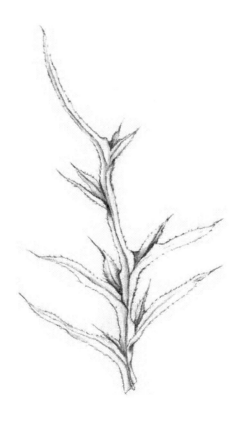

ASHES

Trees held out their arms, securing our descent down the steep embankment to the narrow rocky shore below. The cold lake, held behind a glacial moraine, was teal blue, and mirror smooth. Our eyes scanned the scene. Perfect. Four submerged rocks the size of melons formed cardinal points on the compass with a hollow at the center. This would be the portal. Feather-like ripples lapped at our toes as we stood making offerings and prayers to the once raven-haired beauty who had loved all things classic and the man whose hair had turned white at age eighteen. He'd spent a lifetime on mountains, lakes and rivers, and I wondered if he'd ever paddled by this beautiful spot. And I hoped this place would be amenable to her.

We bent low over the hollow between the rocks and surrendered their ashes to the crystal clear lake as a requiem of bird and water sounds played in the air. The largest particles of ash sank quickly out of sight as can the heaviest times in our lives, and the lightest ash floated angelically for a moment and then slipped beneath the surface, spreading into a delicate milky haze. Slowly and resolutely, it moved out into the eternity of the lake just as two white butterflies, in unison, flew from the east, the direction of wisdom and understanding, to the west, the direction of strength and courage. Perhaps, at last, a reconciliation.

7

LIVE IT SIMPLE

AS YOU GO

A wave departing the sea,
skittering to the shore,
imagines it's the source
of salt and propulsion.

A wave of light falling on a speck of earth,
sprouting a greenling,
imagines it's the source
of warmth and wisdom.

Run from the narrow world
drowning in glitter, gadgets, and noise
as it rushes to make you forget who you are,
snaring the unwary under monuments of calculated distractions
imagining it's the source of fulfillment and love.

Widen into larger worlds of ideas
through doorways of curiosity,
discovering nuggets of passion within yourself
for what you love.
Share them
and give them away,
leaving fragrant breezes
as you go.

WINTER SPELLS

Winter spells reveal subterranean churn
with restless nights and
mischief-playing scenarios
like box office reruns.

For a long time,
life can feel like silk,
but what is smooth inevitably turns to rough
with causes wearing subtle faces—
so best ask what lies hidden,
if not festering beneath.

If time is given space,
quantum threads coalesce to form new unions,
weaving vital ways forward
designed, like a new coat, to fit.

CONSIDER THIS

Consider this—
   everything
     you've learned and lived,
       dreamed and seen, touched and felt,
        brings you to this moment—

you are a wave arriving.
   Within you is an ocean
     embracing the great expanse
      that you are.

This pivotal moment unites
   all that has moved you forward,
     so it is no accident you are here,
      doing what you are doing,
       living what you are living.

An expedition of moments
   brings you to this one—
     you are completely connected.
      You fit right here,
       right now.

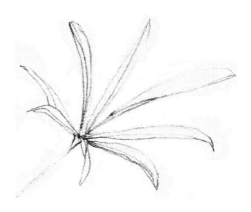

IT'S NOT MY WORK

"It's not my work," she said,
when a letter arrived, offering her a job in Seattle.

"It's not my work," she said,
when a retiring weaver offered a good loom for free.

"It's not my work," she said,
when her mother advocated a Ph.D. in archeology.

Instead,
she fed all things to hunger her instincts.
When a certain translucency
moved through her like a warm breeze,
finding a settling place,
she knew it as truth.

No one knew why she chose as she did—
only the poets,
the mountains,
and the wind.

PLACE OF KINDLY WORDS

There are trajectories,
like roads,
traversing between now
and what will be
as if they know,
but do not tell,
of a realm
meandering
between them.

Could we travel there together,
you and I—
between the lines and illusions,
beneath the details
and divisions—
to the
place
of
kindly
words?

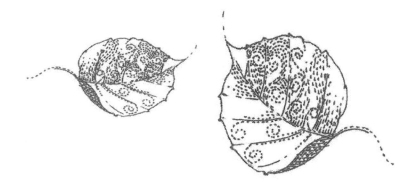

LIVE IT SIMPLE

Live it simple,
with a humility of words and
fewer kneejerk objections.
Make more yeses
with fewer offenses taken,
and know that when red turns to purple,
no forgiveness is too small to be gifted,
no kindness too slim
to be withheld.

8

THE MUSE:
MORE AIR THAN EARTH

YOU'D THINK WE WERE CAMPFIRES

You'd think we were campfires,
the way our brightness pulses and flickers
as we sit in our she-circles
with hands dancing in the air,
sketching our thoughts and
working the clay,

talking of where we've been
and how we've been shaped
like we shape this red-brown earth
with our moist moving hands,
our stories unfurling like flames
stretching us into more than we know—

the clay taking form,
the forms taking us
to places we've never been
before.

INNER SPACE

Inner space,
fertile and rotund,
a gathering just short of taking form,
not ripe enough to stretch into coherency,
taffy still in the pulling stage—
a pregnant sweetness
not yet congealed to wholeness
of what is waiting to become—
a delicate time,
not to be spoken of
too soon.

MORE AIR THAN EARTH

porcelain   more air   than earth

rising   translucent   floating

white   as moonflowers   in moonlight

edges weaving   shadows waving   intimate

bright   as angel trumpets

more air   than earth

COMING HOME TO A POEM

A poem
is comfortable
with paradox and innuendo,
inviting you to peer curiously,
if not hesitantly,
inside—

allowing you to lean into it
though one foot
might remain
outside the door,
until
you see yourself in its mirror
and a bell within you rings—

and it is then,
and only then,
you step over the threshold
to find yourself at home
reaching for the light—
and this is when,
and only when,
you discover
the lamp has forever changed,
casting new colors
about the place—

and this is why,
so wondrously why,
you discover
the rooms have become
so many fulsome
prisms
of light.

AORTAL LIGHT

Held within the crimson skin of the heart bud,
aortal light emits the fragrance of inspiration,
　　　floating,
　　　　　rounded,
　　　　　　　vowel like—
　　　　　　　　　discovered in a flash of recognition.

In a pause,
I sense the Muse,
　　　her ethereal presence
　　　　　on wings,
　　　　　　　glistening.

The creation comes smoothly now and flies
with all its squirm and satin,
　　　congealing into coherence,
　　　　　opaque and transparent all at once—
　　　　　　　an entity in full blossom.

HOW SLIVER THIN

How sliver thin
the words must be
to slip through diaphanous veils
that weave between what we see and what we can't,
to probe the pulsing birthing ground
from which all things arise
that so, in time,
the Muse
might come.

RAISE A FINGER TO YOUR LIPS

Raise a finger to your lips,
for what you refrain from expressing too soon,
and out loud,
keeps receptivity open to the Muse,
who lives
within that generative space
just beyond the mind.

CAUTION, YOU'VE ENTERED A CLAY CONSTRUCTION ZONE

Caution, you've entered a clay construction zone,
and what you are constructing is you.
Come, seize the journey.
Each turn is a new adventure,
suggesting you leave the old map of trepidations behind.

You won't see your world the same again—
the texture on the soles of your shoes,
a pine cone or a simple stick,
a thimble, a button, a kitchen tool, or bracelet.

An untrimmable Muse
lives within each bag of moist, velvet clay,
taking you to undiscovered places.
She'll work on you, visiting your dreams,
greeting you unrelentingly in the morning.
She'll open you, asking you to be more accepting
of the differences you find in others
and the paradoxes that live within yourself.

Slow down, watch.
Take the curves she throws, mindfully.
Proceed in nano-time,
for what sits in front of you
is what you are in the moment.

She is your mirror.
If you are impatient, she may break.
If you drift or feel inadequate, she will bear the scars.
She comes alive with your respect,
and she tears with your haste.
She is tough love.

She likes to play and takes the lead when you let her,
coaxing you into unknown places,

showing you that her nature is your own
in all your many colors.
She is shy, this Muse,
traveling best when judgment is suspended—
blossoming then, shining then,
for all she responds to is you in the moment,
not what others will think tomorrow.

She is surprise and disappointment,
and she will sit with you until you try again,
and then again, and
in the end,
she is joy.

She is a messenger,
and the message is you.

THE POTTER

This clay,
wet and slick,
rises slowly, spinning,
easing upward under pressure
from patient hands
that shape the undulating body
like a lover,
in rhythms swelling and spiraling outward
like datura blossoms on diaphanous summer nights,
aligning to an image
within the heart of the Muse,
who breathes and sings this earthen flesh
as it collars in for the lip
that will host a half-domed lid
for the rising mizusashi,
which, in time,
will hold cool, fresh water—
but first
the agony by fire.
For now,
    the earth
        just
            spins.

9

WE PRINCELINGS

WE PRINCELINGS

Silken fibers weave and swell
these pillows we princelings sit upon,
sipping our liquid gold at high noon,
with demise a disconnected distance away—
forgetting that trees in their treeing
birth our breathing breath
and suns in their sunning
spew ripe abundances of light
that maintain our holy principalities—
while pools of genetic soup
rush to mend the oozing gashes we tear,
drop
by dripping
drop. . . .

SHE-WHO-WATCHES

She-Who-Watches
skirts the edges of the world,
avoiding conventions
that steer the crowded herd,
knowing the shift will come
in its time. . .

it always does.
She feels it like a rain of thorns
that tear and fall
like sheaves
of breaking glass. . .

she always does.
She watches warning shadows
on the wall
from paper puppets
shouting paper words. . .

they always do.
She sees the great epoch tilt,
as small-minded captains
cast about in disarray,
their night course set,
as She-Who-Watches
prepares the healing herbs
and salve. . .

JUST BREATHE, THEY SAY

"Just breathe," they say,
as you pick your way
through star-studded neon days
spiked with news of iceberg meltdowns
and global tempests of fear.

Buy your way, if you can,
behind barricades and cement facades,
hiding from faceless ones
who peer, just as frightened,
from behind their own tenuous walls—
legions in Trojan horses
waiting for the call.

There's fear afoot,
and too few are speaking
in hopes some god of redemption
will intercede and deliver us into the arms of Athena who,
in her wisdom,
might save us from ourselves,
and so we stare
against the wind.

BLACKTOP

Blacktop cracks,
    meandering in crooked lines and crazy eights,
        silently speak demise, while

Palo Verde flowers drop gold
    into their shadowy recesses,
        canyons to tiny creatures who dare cross the ebony ribbons
            moving dragon-like through desert-killing fields.

When slaughtered in their migrations,
    shivers weave through the web
        as progeny are cast into the oblivion
            of the unborn.

Old mariners told stories of great blankets of parrots
    who darkened skies over the southern gulf, but
        in cities now,
            strips of coiffed and sterile soil
                host calculated patches of green as,

drip by drip,
    living systems, once lush and deliriously wild,
        dwindle to a whimper
            and shrink
                from what we rend
                    and ruin.

MINIONS

Minions
  layer up
    new coats of paint
      in vain attempts
        at salvation,

slaving
  over trifling little ledgers,
    tugging at impotent levers and pulleys
      in hopes of saving
        the sagging, sullied
          fortress walls, even

as their tainted citadels
  crack and fall away anyway—
    their rusty stories
      clanging

in beguiling boil,
  blind to their hollow-eyed faces and empty slogans
    shouted from paper pulpits,
      the next one and the next,

the inconceivable conceived—
  arriving in waves
    with crests rising
      just before the trough as

unsung samaritans move at tempered pace
  through trash-littered alleyways and crowded streets—
    no page to their names—
      working the grand procession, while

once again,
  wild things
    with seeds
      tucked in fur and wiry feather clefts
        watch and wait to plant again.

10

ORIGINS

WOMEN WE

Women we—
moon weavers
and kindred keepers,
circle makers and
hunters of seeds and roots
for the roasting fires,
wearing children on hips
like jewels in the sun.

Women we—
listeners for cries in the night,
believers in hope for the morning,
picking up the pieces
and the tent
and the tribe,
sweeping up the ashes,
and washing away the bitters.

Women we—
warriors
fending off the onslaughts,
suffering the tyrannies
with muscles of forbearance and
the resilience of spring,
keepers of the beauty way
in the ghostly freeze of winter.

Women we—
blood red with life,
pulsing with new flesh,
weaving the pod
and rocking the ancestors
with their new face to the wind,
painting in the eyes and filling out the tongues,
bracing for the circle arriving.

Women we—
wisdom keepers,
seers of the inner world,
instinctive stewards with ears to the earth,
rooting out the stale and obsolete,
holding brave fingers to the steely wind,
sensing the shifts
before they arrive.

Women we—
patient when we must,
daring when pushed to the wall,
bearing truth like lanterns in the night
until the silent turning when
the Great Wheel moves
to welcome back the sun
for another season of planting.

Women we—
keepers of the seven directions,
collectors of sacred herbs
and fragrant singing stories
with grace like dancing waters,
shining, shining—
dusting off the stars
so they won't go out.

MEN WE

Men we—
seeking horizons and purpose-driven,
building the walls and determined 'til risen;
knapping the arrows and tanning the leathers,
we carry on shoulders
our children like feathers.

Guarding the camp and protecting the tribe,
standing our ground, safeguarding the lives;
leery of portent and wary of change,
we're courageous and daring,
fun-loving ingrained.   .

Judicious in storms and artful in war,
our minds and muscles flexed to explore;
we question unknowns, create mighty buffers,
to succeed is a must
in the eyes of our brothers.

With instincts to hold and know-how to mend,
our groins heated and driven and anxious to spend;
we're men we, we're proud we, self-sufficient and strong,
we're tender, contained,
and need to belong.

Respecting the space for womanly ways
as they move and measure a mysterious maze;
we honor their cycles, their circles arriving,
drumming and chanting
for children surviving.

Instinctive of herds stealthily moving,
observing the suns and always improving;
marking the seasons with rock, blood and bone,
assessing the changes
best done when alone.

Telling our stories, retelling the tales,
perceiving their wisdom, dissecting the vails;
forging the hours like tools to survive
so by all that we live for
we'll grow and we'll thrive.

Wisdom is sought from the finest of mentors,
our hearts and minds seeking to enter;
some bleed from father-wounds like nails to the bone,
hoping and healing
and hunting for home.

11

REFLECTIONS ON COLOR

BLUE

Blue
can come as a cold surprise,
filling empty spaces if you let it,
coaxing the sadness out
when you don't need it anymore.

Blue
cleans the hollow bone of your soul
if you make an appeal.
Ebullient, ubiquitous,
blue light special blue,
you sing it when you're on your knees
and down on your luck;
you admire it when it's true enough;
you fly in it, swim in it,
this color of forever;
a surround sound
that rocks you into birth
and waits patiently for you to die
many times
before you're through.
Mysterious, unrestrainable,
irresistible, inexorable,
almighty
blue ribbon
blue.

RED

Red
splits you in two
when it finds you sleeping
with such velocity
that reason fails,
like slipping off the Red Road,
shattering you
into fearsome neon splinters
that pierce and drain your soul
of any semblance
of what was once your life.

Red
bleeds hot crimson rivers of war,
taking you home,
if you're lucky,
where compassion draws you back
into the womb of her arms,
softening the shade to flesh,
where life began and you begin again.

Red
greets you on the porch at sunset
with its offspring and distant relatives,
and it is then you know your broken pieces
are connected by indelible threads
making whole again
the ceremonial cycle
of your life.

YELLOW

Yellow
immodestly parades on flowers
and unabashedly inhabits suns,
but rarely overtakes territories
governed by blues and greens
except in the morning
when she reigns like a queen,
rising from the night.

Yellow
illuminates with a fearless soul,
shooting headlong into black like a star,
piercing small-mindedness
with brilliant hot clarion calls,
opening sleepwalkers
to the juice of gold.

PURPLE

Purple
loves you anyway,
so stand by your journey,
and she will pick you up
regardless of where you've been
or where you're going.

Purple
garnishes you
in the sweep of her royal velvet,
speaking at midnight in amethyst tones,
cradling you in your quivering hours,
singing you back to yourself.

Purple
splashes herself sparingly,
even among feathers,
slipping quietly inward
so be watchful,
for she holds mysteries
that can't be overestimated
once she sets her course—
a formidable force
to be reckoned with,
like love.

ORANGE

Orange
is often forgotten
but ignores this slight
with noisy delight
at being alive
in spring
when poppies bloom
and leaves explode with fire
on bright autumn afternoons
as pumpkins come in from the fields
wearing toothy grins and ghoulish faces.

Orange
concedes to no one
except its parents,
the reds and yellows,
which it regards
as masters of the universe.
And who can match
the succulent sweetness
of a hot peach pie
in summertime?

GREEN

Green
brings you back
to the breast of the Earth,
who springs you into summers
and falls you into winters and,
when fully spent,
cradles your body within the pungent,
moss-green fields of her skin
until, at last,
you emerge into the greening
of another
time.

BLACK

Black
is a clever paradox,
a kaleidoscopic shape-shifter
that at once contains every
thing
and no
thing
at all.

Black
obscures the sacred,
yet births the most sacred of all
with its resplendent endlessness.
When spent with absorption
into black holes and hungry hearts,
it ignites new worlds
into life.

Black
spreads dust-strewn cloaks of darkness
over boundless galaxies
but hidden within lie all possibilities,
an alchemical synthesis
waiting to be born.

Black
holds the darkest of memories
reminding us that we are partners
to our own resurrection
from which
only light
can come.

WHITE

White
hunts you down
to pick you up,
seeks you out
to bring you into her expanse,
shattering your isolation until,
transfigured,
you recognize
your connectedness.

White,
an alchemy of light,
mends your separate parts,
transforming each
into a nexus of hidden manna
of such proportion
your new name
can be written.

White
asks you to raise a flag of surrender
when you discover
you are but a spark
amid the endless sum
of her parts.

White
brings you home to the cosmic core
through a symphony of opposites
where there is no fear
for there's nothing
she doesn't already
contain.

12

A COLLECTION
of
HAIKU AND SENRYU

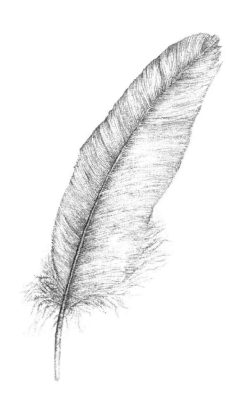

MEDITATIONS AND CONTEMPLATIONS

The faintest of sounds
cause smooth subtle inner waves—
earth body speaking!

We journal the sun,
it will rise up anyway—
time concedes to truth.

Lost in subtle breath,
return to clear hidden spring—
mountain is waiting.

When you are ready,
rake falling leaves many times—
the teacher will come.

Deep, still listening,
all agendas set aside—
clear blue sky opens.

Fertile stream of *now*
where all things come to commune—
past, present, future.

Now is illusive,
a ripple in the streaming—
feel immensity!

Troubled heart opens,
breathing rides the silver waves—
soft stillness returns.

Inexorably,
energy now converging
expands into white.

Great equalizer—
there are no eloquent words,
just bubbles rising.

Immutable wind,
what is this that breathes me in,
breathes me out again?

Restless surly winds,
succulence remains hidden—
thoughts squeeze out the juice.

Inner garden root
watches winds twist and tumble—
clear fountain splashes.

Stillness charged with life,
inner quanta resonate—
silent music plays.

SPRING

Sweet spring came and went—
waited weeks for yesterday,
now today it's gone.

Dark thundercloud swells,
restless crucible of rain—
kitchen for flowers!

Planted seeds of kale
imagining a salad—
something found them first.

What was annoyance
now turns to effortlessness—
winter precedes spring.

Winged ones still know
there must have been a first sun—
it rose like thunder!

From clutch of winter,
spring takes measure of the task—
a grand leap of faith!

A sprouting of seeds,
promises in the making—
a small bird watches.

Lifting a faint scent,
ghost on an early spring breeze—
the high desert blooms.

Night slips into the marsh,
bouquets of stars float east to west—
stealth maneuver of fur.

SUMMER

Serene shining trees
without malice or drama—
no names. . . .no stories.

Ravens are leaving,
summer fields lush to the north—
the whole desert tilts.

Fragrance of roses—
but there are none in the yard!
Pale breath of heaven.

Fragile moonflowers—
quiescent white shimmering,
stillness breathes the air.

Young loon bobs on lake,
mist at dawn luminous gold—
small boat sneaks from shore.

Falling like a star,
spider drops on silver thread—
Limos is hungry.

Summer zucchini
hides beneath the juicy leaves—
catch them when they're young!

Desert morning breeze,
waves of Maine on Norcross Pond—
doves replace the loons.

Bees are mostly gone,
silence lurks on every bloom—
flowers unfulfilled.

It rose untethered
floating high into the blue—
a ripe summer seed.

Late fading summer
brings the slow contented sounds—
life's rush is over.

Flowers now in bloom
hold seeds of dissolution—
summer turns to dust.

AUTUMN

Leaves wither and fold,
one final flower blossoms—
spring is in disguise.

White crane on wet rock,
autumn's meadow tea glides by—
small fish disappears.

Drifting autumn clouds
carry waves of canyon drumming—
dry land drinks the mist.

Obese autumn clouds—
dark canteens spilling their fruit,
dry land is tickled.

Old door blows open,
for a moment wind enters—
red splash of cold leaves.

Green mammatus clouds,
a wickedness of silence—
dash to the cellar!

WINTER

All things come and go,
compassion thus arises—
winter bears the fruit.

Stoic mystery,
winter mountain solitude—
a cold refreshment of. . . .still.

Green midwinter fly
plays thin legs like a fiddle—
spring will come too late.

Trees black, stark and bare
like hairs on winter mountains—
time to wax the skis!

I knew you were there
by the whisper of your step—
a smother of snow.

"Why go there," he asked,
"gloom and chill are everywhere?"
There might fly a bird!

ANOTHER KIND OF WINTER

Grandpa labored hard,
drove wagons of crops to town—
orphan boys can't cry.

Shrapnel tears the night,
branches shatter, leaves scatter—
old man sits and rocks.

He lies motionless,
a wise man of many years—
someone slams the door.

Softly he lay down
under an old sturdy oak—
white cloud drifts away.

Once upon a time
there was a story that grew—
mighty myth tightens.

Hot black tea steeping
in a white porcelain cup—
hordes plunder the town.

A noose of black thread
around the neck of a fly—
some things never change.

Feet up in a chair,
birds roosting high in their nests—
thundercloud coming.

THOUGHTS CONSIDERED

Bright moon parts the clouds,
pure silver water falling—
traffic far away.

It is possible—
between shrill traffic noises,
a whisper of still.

Predawn sky brightens,
in hushed silence we face east—
soft river of wind.

Slipping out early
under thin mask of darkness—
sunrise chrysalis.

Blood-red eclipse glides,
auspicious full moon labors—
eerie darkness spreads.

Red cloud on mountain,
sunset dragon moving north—
time to run for home!

Snaking into town,
red taillights on the highway—
warm bed waits ahead.

At the borderland,
at the very razor's edge,
a stealth sliver shifts.

Marauding skunks raid,
pots and pans clang through the camps,
moon throws green shadows.

Mischief in the yard,
furry masked bandits plunder—
a knock on the door.

Mirror on the wall,
for many years it watches—
spring turns to winter.

Close over my head
a circle of ravens spin—
a gladness of wings.

Stitching the pieces,
tending vital connections—
she does endings well.

Time plays heady tricks—
that which we are moving toward
has already come.

Sometimes it sweeps through
like a cold shoulder of wind—
great shiver of loss.

When you slipped away,
I walked the edge of the sea—
my eyes are now yours.

Small cloud in big sky
formed by water from the lake—
we are not alone.

Ancient ones left rocks,
now rubble piles in the field,
pointing to the sun.

Tell your stories true,
only some will hear your dreams—
you were born for this.

Model the lessons,
provide little to resist,
prepare for surprise.

Flash of neon green,
quintessential memory—
sunrise on Maui.

White lotus floating
over black still pond at night—
fish stares at the moon.

IT WAS ALL FOR LOVE

I
I came home tired.
He sat sweetly as I napped,
watching every breath.

II
When in the shower,
he plays his wooden flute.
I melt to chocolate.

III
So good to be home,
this place where everything fits,
this place of soft sheets.

IV
What was it all for?
It seemed so complicated then—
it was all for love.

ABOUT THE AUTHOR

Pamala Ballingham was born in Oakland, California, and grew up near Albany, New York. She and her husband, Tim Ballingham, live in the high Sonoran Desert of Tucson, Arizona. When Pamala experienced the grandeur and noble silence of the high desert and red rock canyon lands, her internal world shifted. The ambiance of these pristine landscapes continue to influence her music, visual art, and poetry. Pamala practices meditation, and she studied the profoundly serene and complex art of Japanese tea ceremony.

For decades she and her husband have closely connected with the culture and spiritual traditions of Native Americans. Whenever possible, they quietly sit around campfires listening to wise elders tell their stories and, when appropriate, participate in ceremonies. Most of the elders, the fragile vessels of the old ways, are gone, but their lessons continue to weave themselves into Pamala's creative work.

She enjoys working with plants and loves animals. She once rescued a hatchling Inca Dove blown from its nest in a storm and then lived with "Birdie" for twelve fascinating years. She volunteered at a small animal rehabilitation center, experiencing with delight and wonder the spirit of each recuperating resident.

Pamala and Tim cofounded Earth Mother Productions, which produced several national award-winning recordings: *Earth Mother Lullabies from Around the World* (Volumes 1, 2, and 3), *Treasury of Earth Mother Lullabies* (compilation of three volumes), *Magical Melodies from Broadway and Motion Pictures*, and *Voyage for Dreamers,* a collection of her own songs as well as two songs by her friend, the late Kate Wolf. Some of the accolades received are several American Library Association's Notable Children's Recording awards and Parents' Choice "Best of the Best Bedtime Music." Her music appears on several recordings produced by Sony Music Entertainment: *Lullabies and Bedtime Stories* and *Baby B' Gosh Lullabies*.

Pamala directed a treatment program for adults with serious mental illnesses in Tucson, and she has been a full-time studio artist. Her work has included the creation of sculpted clay neckpieces and, with Tim, large clay wall art. The neckpieces were exhibited by the late fashion designer, Edith Head, and sold by the Kruger Van Eerde Gallery on Madison Avenue in New York and Neiman Marcus in Dallas, Texas. They also appeared in the *Goodfellow Catalog of Wonderful Things*. Pamala and Tim's wall art was featured in the book *Beautiful Things*, and *Four Seasons* was purchased for McGraw Hill Publishing Company's permanent collection.

Pamala earned a bachelor's degree in art education, and a master's degree in counseling. She and Tim give experiential workshops and teach classes using clay as a means to encourage people to explore their fascinating inner world of creativity.

Connect with Pamala Ballingham across the Internet –
Facebook: https://www.facebook.com/EarthMotherProductions
LinkedIn: https://www.linkedin.com/in/pamala-ballingham-029a60167
YouTube channel: Pamala Ballingham
Society6.com/EarthMotherProductions
Email: EarthMotherProductions@gmail.com
Postal Mail: Earth Mother Productions
                PO Box 43204
                Tucson, AZ 85733